Mamie Eisenhower

Wife, Mother, First Lady:

Her Impact and Influence on Her Time

The Eisenhower Seminar
Eisenhower National Historic Site
Gettysburg, Pennsylvania

Library of Congress Catalog Card Number: 98-70448

Copyright ©1998 by Eisenhower National Historic Site

ISBN 0-9663741-0-X

Preface

An individual's success is often the result of the support provided by others. During their 53 years of marriage, Mamie Doud Eisenhower was the primary person who provided the support for the success of Dwight D. Eisenhower. Whether during his military career, his political career, or in retirement, Mamie was there to provide the support and the foundation that Ike needed. She was very much an individual in her own right. A trendsetter in fashion during the presidential years, and a quiet champion of worthy causes including civil rights, Mamie Eisenhower was a notable First Lady.

On the occasion of the centennial of her birth, the Eisenhower National Historic Site in cooperation with Gettysburg College, the Dwight D. Eisenhower Society, and Eastern National Park & Monument Association sponsored an Eisenhower Seminar. This seminar, "Mamie D. Eisenhower — Wife, Mother, First Lady: Her Impact and Influence on Her Time," was held November 9, 1996 at the Cyclorama Center of Gettysburg National Military Park. Five notable historians, Susan Eisenhower, Carol Hegeman, Karal Ann Marling, Edith Mayo, and Michael J. Birkner, presented papers and engaged in discussion about the achievements of Mamie Eisenhower.

The proceedings of this Seminar place the accomplishments of Mamie Eisenhower in the context of her life as the wife of one of the most influential Americans of the twentieth century, and in the context of the role of women in American society at the century's apex.

James C. Roach
Site Manager
Eisenhower National Historic Site
December 1996

3

Featured Speakers

Susan Eisenhower is the author of *Mrs. Ike: Memories and Reflections on the Life of Mamie Eisenhower.* Her previous book, *Breaking Free*, was a personal account of high level American - Soviet politics during glasnost, and her relationship with her husband, Russian space scientist, Ronald Sagdeev. Ms. Eisenhower is President of The Eisenhower Group, a Washington based international consulting firm, and chairperson of The Center for Post-Soviet Studies. She is a recognized expert on the former Soviet Union, and regularly contributes news analysis on foreign affairs for TV, radio, and newspapers.

Dr. Karal Ann Marling is Professor of Art History and American Studies at the University of Minnesota. She is the author of a wide range of books on American art and cultural history including *Edward Hopper*, and *Graceland: Going Home With Elvis.* Her 1994 study of style and material culture, *As Seen on TV: The Visual Culture of Everyday Life in the 1950s* was named a *New York Times* Book of the Year. She has curated many exhibits of American art throughout the U.S. and Canada, and is currently working on a biography of Norman Rockwell and on an international exhibit of Disney created architecture.

Edith P. Mayo is curator in the Division of Political History at the National Museum of American History. She has worked for over twenty years as a public historian at the Smithsonian Institution, and is active in collecting for the Museum's holdings. She has curated major exhibitions on women's history, politics, and civil rights, including a complete reconception of the Smithsonian's famous First Ladies exhibit entitled, *First Ladies: Political Role and Public Image.* She is editor of *The Smithsonian Book of the First Ladies.* Her published articles include, *Be a Party Girl: Campaign Appeals to Women in the 1950s.*

Carol A. Hegeman is the supervisory historian at Eisenhower National Historic Site where she has been interpreting the life of the Eisenhowers since 1980. She has conducted extensive research into the life and work of both the President and First Lady, including over 200 hours of oral history interviews. She is the author of *Thaw in the Cold War: Eisenhower and Khrushchev at Gettysburg,* a lesson plan in the Teaching With Historic Places series published by the National Trust for Historic Preservation. Ms. Hegeman was named 1991 NFS Regional Interpreter of the Year.

5

Mamie Eisenhower In Perspective

Carol A. Hegeman

Mamie Doud Eisenhower was born 100 years ago this Thursday. She was the last First Lady born in the 19th century. Her upbringing and her view on life were reflected in how she perceived and carried out her role as First Lady. Mamie had life experiences to which American women related. As we will learn today, her years as an Army wife shaped her thinking on her relationship with her husband and family. She had lived in difficult places. She and Ike had lost their first son at age three and a half. They endured long separations. All of these events strained their marriage. Yet as Susan Eisenhower will discuss, the Eisenhowers' marriage endured.

After World War II, American women left the work place, whether by choice or societal pressures, to stay home in large numbers and raise the baby boom generation. As housewives, American women found Mrs. Eisenhower a role model, whether she was supporting her husband on the campaign trail or dressing in the fashions of the time. Our other speakers, Edith Mayo and Karal Ann Marling, will address each of these topics. But in remembering Mamie today, I'd like to look at a more personal side of her, her personality.

One of my favorite quotes by Mamie Doud Eisenhower is recounted by Julie Nixon Eisenhower in her book *Special People*. It was the 1972 inaugural parade for President Nixon's second term. Mrs. Eisenhower was riding in the same car as Julie. As Mamie said, she was "playing David" while David Eisenhower, Julie's husband, was off in the Navy. As Julie timidly waved at the crowd lining the street, Mamie said, "Don't give them any of that prissy stuff. Give them a big wave. Really say hello."[1] That's the Mamie Eisenhower that 1950s Americans knew and admired.

Her son, John, called her a westerner and said "she was rather quite friendly and outgoing, especially with strangers." [2] She had a warm, open, breezy personality that he attributed to her years growing up in the west. Mamie was born in Boone, Iowa, and grew up in Denver, Colorado. The Doud Family was close knit. Though they socialized among their close circle of friends, the family spent a lot of time together. Within this close circle, Mamie's personality blossomed. Though an average student in high school, Mamie went on to Miss Walcott's finishing school in Denver, learning poise, etiquette, and how to manage a household.

Mrs. Eisenhower was a traditionalist in her role as wife and mother. She always said there could only be one star in the Eisenhower family, and it wasn't her.[3] When asked if she wished she'd had a career, she responded. "I had a career. His name was Ike."[4]

That career began in the fall of 1915 in San Antonio, Texas. The well-to-do Doud family spent winters in San Antonio. One day, while the Doud family was visiting friends at Fort Sam Houston, Lt. Eisenhower in his first assignment after graduating from West Point, was doing his rounds as Officer of the Guard. The mutual friend called Eisenhower over to introduce him to the Doud family. Eisenhower was reluctant to come, but finally was convinced. You see, Ike had the reputation as the post woman hater. He later said that it wasn't that he didn't like women, it was that he couldn't afford women. Eisenhower was immediately taken with the petite Mamie Doud and asked her to walk post with him. As they walked by the barracks he would tell her to look away, she might see something she shouldn't. But with a mind of her own, Mamie took it all in. Eisenhower later wrote "The one who attracted my eye instantly was a vivacious and attractive girl, smaller than average, saucy in the look about her face and her whole attitude. I was intrigued by her appearance."[5] For her part, Mamie said that Ike was "a bruiser, not like some of those lounge lizards she dated."[6]

By the time they completed the walk, Eisenhower was smitten. He tried to get a date, but Mamie was very popular. She was booked for the next three Saturdays, so he asked her for the fourth. In the afternoons or while Mamie was out

Mamie in wedding dress, July 1916. (Dwight D. Eisenhower Library)

with other young men, Ike sat on the porch with her parents and got to know them. Then when Mamie was dropped off by her date, Ike was also there to say good night. Soon Ike and Mamie were dating each other exclusively. By Valentine's Day they were engaged, and they were married July 1, 1916. Mamie's career as Ike's wife lasted 53 years.

Early in her married life, Mamie learned the importance of home. She saw her role as providing a comfortable place for her husband to come home to. Now this was especially challenging when the Eisenhowers lived in Gettysburg in 1918. During this time Captain Eisenhower had his first independent command as commander of Camp Colt, a tank training corps for 10,000 men located just west of the Cyclorama Center on the fields of Pickett's Charge. In the seven months Mamie and their first son, Doud Dwight, were in Gettysburg, the family lived in three different places. Of her arrival in Gettysburg, Mamie remembers,

> It was raining to beat the band. And Ike had one of his aides meet me and took me to this little place he had rented, which has a window in the front and a window in the back. No circulation, no heat. A coal stove. I'd never seen a coal stove in my life. I didn't know what to do. And the only heat you had was a base burner in the living room that heated the bedroom above, period.... So we lived in this very strange house and then during the summer months they let us stay in the ATO fraternity house which was right next door. But we could only stay in there during the summer. It had the most beautiful ballroom and no kitchen, so I, who'd never washed any dishes or done anything like that, had to wash dishes in the bath tub. Ike bought me a two-burner oil stove, and I was frightened to have to light it, I was afraid it'd blow up. So, I'd have to wait for him to come home to light it. I was twenty years old, twenty-one years old: I knew nothing about any of these things. So it was really pretty rugged. So then when the school season started, ... there was a little house on Springs Avenue .... and that was the last house we lived in. And while we're in there I got the news that my sister, who's younger than myself, had

died, so I got right on the train and went to Denver. And then Ike was moved to Fort Benning, Georgia. So I never saw my things again. And one of them.. the baby's high chair never showed up. I don't know whatever happened to it.[7]

Mamie's moves with the military encouraged her frugality when managing the household finances. Eisenhower always turned his pay check over to her. She said "I was the one that kept him out of debt. Ike didn't know whether he had 5 cents or 10 cents and he couldn't have cared less."[8] She made one mistake in the early years. Before moving someone convinced her to sell all her furniture and buy new when she got to the new post. She soon learned that she could not replace her old furniture with the money she got for it.[9] Forever after she made careful decisions with money. In 1933, when the banks were going to close, Mamie withdrew the family savings and purchased a couch. Today that couch is in the living room of the Eisenhower home here in Gettysburg. Mrs. Eisenhower just had it slipcovered to go with the new decor. An antique Sheraton chest of drawers in the master bedroom was also a prized possession. Mamie said it took her two years to save the money to get it. As she said, "I think so much more of those things that I worked hard for..." [10]

It was during those frugal years in the military that Mamie developed into a true hostess. The Eisenhower home always seemed to be the place where all the officers and their wives gathered. Dinners were potluck. For entertainment, Mamie would play the piano. She played all the popular songs of the day by ear as their friends gathered around for a sing-along. Soon the Eisenhowers' quarters were known as Club Eisenhower. As Eisenhower rose in rank, the breadth of Mrs. Eisenhower's entertaining expanded. By the time the Eisenhowers' were in the Philippines in the late 1930s, Mrs. Eisenhower was regularly entertained at the Presidential palace. Her experience and knowledge of etiquette even carried over into her family life. The Eisenhower grandchildren all confess that they all learned the proper use of the finger bowl by age three.[11]

Mamie's experience as a hostess was especially useful as

First Lady. She and the President entertained extensively during their years in the White House. She was personally involved in selecting the menus and making up guest lists and seating arrangements. The types of events varied widely, from stag dinners which were men only events for the President and close friends, to State dinners, to receptions for the many clubs and organizations anxious to meet the First Lady.

Mary Jane McCaffrey Monroe, Mrs. Eisenhower's White House social secretary, recounts Mamie greeting a group from Kensington, Maryland.

> Mrs. Eisenhower had already shaken hands with about three or four hundred or more ladies. But there was one particular lady who stayed 'til the very last. She was the end one in line. And she went through and Mrs. Eisenhower shook her hands and said, 'What? You here again?' She had a fantastic memory for names and for faces, and apparently this lady, and she told me this later on herself, she said,"I was in here about three weeks ago and I bet my friend that she wouldn't remember me."[12]

Mrs. Eisenhower especially liked to decorate the White House for the holidays. This hobby probably stems from her girlhood, because her parents always enjoyed decorating for all the holidays. She decorated the White House with corn stalks, pumpkins and black cats for Halloween, and eggs and bunnies for Easter, but she went all out for Christmas. She had the hallways filled with poinsettias with white branches sticking out. The entrance way columns were wrapped in garlands of pine with big red bows. Small Christmas trees flanked the East room fireplaces. In the State Dining Room, wreaths hung from the candelabra. And giant Christmas trees stood in the East Room, the Blue Room and even outside on the North Portico. As White House Chief Usher J. B. West said, "Mamie Eisenhower decked the halls with more than holly."[13]

Mamie was the first First Lady to have an official staff. According to Mary Jane McCaffrey Monroe, Mrs. Eisenhower's secretary in the White House Social Office, Mamie was so popular as First Lady that she received five or six thousand letters a week. That number would escalate to

10,000 letters a week for birthdays and anniversaries. In describing her popularity, McCaffrey Monroe said, "People felt something about her. They felt toward her like a next door neighbor."[14] Mrs. Eisenhower insisted that every letter get a response and many of them received a personal letter from her.

The personal interest that Mrs. Eisenhower took in answering correspondence was also evident in her relationship with the White House staff. She knew everyone by name and often engaged them in conversation about their personal lives. Her interest in their family was reflected each year at Christmas as she presented the staff with Christmas presents she personally selected. She also sent presents for spouses and children. She also remembered their birthdays and made sure to have a cake baked to celebrate the occasion. The degree of personal interest she took in the staff is perhaps best illustrated in the picnics the Eisenhowers held here in Gettysburg. For the Eisenhower's 39th wedding anniversary, they hosted a picnic at the farm. Invitations went out to all staff members whether working on the President's staff or the domestic staff. Everyone had an opportunity to tour the Eisenhower's newly completed home and stroll the grounds.

As First Lady, Mamie didn't adopt a cause as others have done. Nor did she actively get involved in the business of the Presidency. She said she set foot in the Oval office only four times, each time by invitation.[15] But as anyone in a marriage knows, if the husband and wife are a team, each spouse influences the other in many subtle ways. And the Eisenhowers were a team. When Ike composed a prayer for his first inauguration, he consulted Mamie for approval. About his speeches, Mamie said to him one time, "I'm an average person. Now when you make a speech, make it short and don't use big words. We know you know 'em. But use small words like we can understand."[16] She went on to say, "Now I think I was his best subject on that."[17]

By her own calculation the Eisenhowers lived in 37 different homes. Mamie said she lived in every kind of house but an igloo. But it was here in Gettysburg that she and Ike finally had their first and only home. Of the importance of home she said,

Well, home to us meant a great deal, too. Now that I think the American people should know and realize. That it's in the home that everything starts. And ours has always been a home. No matter where we were or what sort of a house we lived in or anything else. Take a few little pictures out, you know, and put around, and little ashtrays or something, and it would turn out to be home.[18]

This idea of home and the home's ability to rejuvenate a person really came through during Eisenhower's illnesses. During the White House years, Ike recuperated at the farm from his heart attack and his ileitis operation. Even near the end, when Eisenhower was in Walter Reed for the last 10 months of his life, Mamie felt that if she could just get him back to the farm to sit on the glass enclosed porch, or walk the fields, that the atmosphere would rejuvenate him.[19] But, of course, that was not to be.

Those years after Ike's death were lonely years. Many of Mrs. Eisenhower's friends were also passing away. At one point David and Julie tried to talk Mamie into moving in with them. She promptly replied that they had their life to live and she had hers. Those last years friends and family still visited the Gettysburg farm. And there was laughter in the house. But it just wasn't the same. Granddaughter Mary Jean remembers a visit about two years after her grandfather died.

The house was full (with guests) and she put me in with her on his side of the bed. And just as we were about to go to sleep she said, "It's nice to have somebody over there. That bed's been so empty." She just kind of cried herself to sleep that night. She really had such a hard time after he died.[20]

But I'd like to end by remembering Mamie Eisenhower in a happier way. The way I think most Americans remember her. During President Nixon's term in office, Mrs. Eisenhower was often included in Nixon family events. Once she spent Easter with the Nixon family at Camp David. For Easter breakfast, the staff had dyed Easter eggs with the names of family members and set them on the table as place cards. Mrs. Eisenhower especially liked to tell how President Nixon's egg said "Mr. President," his wife's said "Mrs. Nixon," but hers just said "Mamie."[21]

1. Eisenhower, Julie Nixon, *Special People*, Simon and Schuster, New York, p. 188.

2. John S. D. Eisenhower, Interview with Carol Hegeman, 1986.

3. Media Transcripts, Inc., Mamie Eisenhower Interview with Barbara Walters, August 30, 1979, p. 41.

4. Eisenhower, Julie Nixon, *Special People*, p. 194.

5. Eisenhower, Dwight D., *At Ease: Stories I Tell To Friends*, Doubleday & Company, Inc., Garden City, New York, p. 113.

6. Eisenhower, Julie Nixon, *Special People*, p. 195.

7. Mamie Eisenhower, Interview with Ed Bearss, August 15, 1973.

8. *Ibid*.

9. Brandon, Dorothy, *Mamie Doud Eisenhower: Portrait of a First Lady*, Charles Scribner's Sons, New York, 1954, p. 89.

10. *Ibid.*

11. Susan Eisenhower, Interview with Carol Hegeman, February 8, 1986.

12. Mary Jane McCaffrey Monroe and Anne Parsons, Interview with Carol Hegeman, September 22, 1983.

13. West, J. B. *Upstairs at the White House*, Warner Books, Inc., New York, 1974, p.170.

14. Mary Jane McCaffrey Monroe and Anne Parsons, Interview with Carol Hegeman, September 22, 1983.

15. Eisenhower, Julie Nixon, *Special People*, p. 203.

16. Mamie Eisenhower, Interview with Ed Bearss, August 15, 1973.

17. *Ibid.*

18. *Ibid.*

19. *Ibid.*

20. Mary Jean Eisenhower, Interview with Carol Hegeman June 25, 1987.

21. Eisenhower, Julie Nixon, *Special People*, p. 215.

Mamie Eisenhower and the Campaign of the 1950s

Edith P. Mayo

Around the turn of the century, prospective First Ladies such as Mary Bryan had appeared with their spouses as they campaigned. Frances Cleveland in the mid-1880s and early 1890s became a campaign symbol in her own right. Even Ida McKinley had a "Women's McKinley Club" in her honor. Eleanor Roosevelt campaigned extensively on her own on her husband's behalf. But it was not until the 1950s that the role of the First Lady as campaigner became institutionalized.[1] That this occurred in the decade of the 1950s was not accidental, but was due to a conjunction of circumstances, not the least of which was the appearance on the political scene of Mamie Eisenhower as the ideal spouse of a candidate.

Factors in this fortuitous conjunction of circumstances included:

- women voting in virtually equal numbers as men;
- Republican advertising men crafting the Eisenhower candidate image, scripting it tightly, and producing a variety of campaign "consumer" products as direct campaign appeals to women;
- the use of "family values" as a major campaign issue;
- Mamie Eisenhower's personality and campaign image fitting this agenda perfectly;
- the translation of campaign issues into "women's" terms;
- the extensive use of women as grassroots party workers and oilers of party machinery at the local level;
- the decision to "run" the wives of the presidential and vice presidential candidates as a means to appeal to women voters.

The fifties marked a turning point in the relationship between women and political parties. By the postwar election of 1952, women had become accustomed to their role as voters and, for the first time in history, now constituted half of the voting electorate. Of the 61.2 million people casting ballots in 1952, 30.9 million were men and 30.3 million were women.[2] The major political parties had to determine how to capture women's ballots. The Republican Party made a particularly concerted and effective effort. Led by Ivy Baker Priest, the assistant chair of the Republican National Committee and head of the party's Women's Division, the Republicans aimed a strong awareness campaign at women voters.[3] Focusing on the fifties themes of women's postwar return to the home and the solidarity of the family as a bulwark against Communism, Republicans, with the help of their advertising executives,[4] successfully translated campaign issues into concepts that appealed to American women.

As women were now an equally important part of the electorate, political parties had a vast new constituency to whom they must appeal for votes. It became extremely important, therefore, to "sell" the candidate to American women. In addition, while most of the party power structure did not encourage women to run as candidates, they did want to use women's time and energies to become grassroots party workers, and they certainly wanted women's votes.

Since the beginning of the twentieth century, advertising men had pitched their wares by creating the concept that women were the consummate American consumers. By extension, in a capitalist economy, the "freedom" to "choose" a product had, for much of the twentieth century, been equated in advertising campaigns to "freedom" politically.[5] Since women as consumers in the marketplace were accustomed to this kind of advertising, the ad men reasoned that "selling" the candidate to women as political consumers was simply the next step. As ad men migrated into the Republican campaign, they began to package their candidates as a commodity to be chosen. The message was clear to women — selecting the best candidate was much like selecting the best product in the marketplace. American political parties had produced and distributed a variety of campaign items with a special appeal for women since the late 1820s, but it was not until the 1950s that a political party launched the first deliberate campaign aimed at women voters. This effort — coming more than thirty years after women won the right to vote — generated a rich array of campaign artifacts that tell us much about attitudes toward women and their role in politics and society during the era of the Cold War.

Republican ad men crafted a series of campaign appeals to women, pitched as advertising to women consumers, translating complicated political issues into terms, as one stated, "that the little lady could understand." In the nineteenth century, before women could vote, partisan politics were often a family affair. The parties produced a variety of campaign consumer products with a direct appeal to women such as sewing boxes, hair brushes and ornaments, jewelry, and ceramic wares for the home that were used by women to reinforce the party loyalties of the family. Women themselves often made political quilts and campaign banners for partisan use. Such personal and domestic items with the candidate's name had appealed to women since their introduction in the political campaigns of the mid-nineteenth century,[6] and vast numbers of such items were offered for sale in the 1950s.

"Family Values" as a campaign issue was a strong theme in both the 1952 and 1956 campaigns. Domestic images were potent because the American public craved stability after the economic chaos of the Great Depression and the devastation of World War II. The return to normal living was symbolized by an emphasis on the home, the traditional family, and traditional, feminine, supportive roles for women. Women were seen as the mainstay of the home, and the strong American family was promoted by all aspects of the culture as a bulwark against the spread of "Godless Communism" during the Cold War atmosphere that pervaded the decade of the 1950s. Mamie Eisenhower's own personality, and the image that she projected of herself both visually and in print, as the adoring wife whose entire identity was consumed by husband and family, fit the 1950s campaign agenda perfectly.

Mamie Eisenhower was an outgoing woman who genuinely loved people. She smiled easily, and was approachable and accessible — perceived as a woman not unlike the average American woman who had been exalted to a high position by the circumstances of her husband's political career. She presented herself as a level-headed, plain-spoken, no-nonsense wife who was utterly devoted to her husband and family. She was willing to do anything to assist and promote Ike. In addition, Mrs. Eisenhower was perceived as decidedly NOT political and, therefore, not a threat to the established political order. She was not in the campaign to promote her own agenda, nor to promote a political or social cause, nor for power, position, or adulation (though, I dare say, she enjoyed those perks that came with the position of First Lady, and knew how to use them). In short, the women of America perceived her as one of their own. She epitomized the popularly-held conventions of femininity in postwar America.

A more visible presence for the candidates' wives in this campaign did not, however, signal a departure from traditional concepts about women's role. Rather, the campaigns and the demeanor of the women tended to reinforce traditional gender ideology. In both presidential elections in the fifties, campaign devices and images of women conveyed time-honored ideals of home and family.[7] Campaign objects with a feminine appeal were circulated in enormous quantities by Republicans in 1952. Household items such as plates, cup and saucer sets, salt and pepper shakers, bud vases, pitchers, cream and sugar sets, plastic measuring spoons, and cast-iron trivets abounded, as did campaign jewelry in the form of necklaces, bracelets, earrings, and pins, all bearing the likeness of the candidate or proclaiming "I Like Ike" in rhinestones. There were Republican emery boards, napkins, mirrors, combs, thimbles, and fans.

Though the silk scarves of the 1888 campaign foreshadowed an appeal to women through wearing apparel, they pale in comparison with the apparel appeal of the 1952 campaign. The well-dressed Republican woman would not leave home without wearing her "I Like Ike" blouse or dress (with full circle skirt, of course), her Republican umbrella, or her "Ike and Dick" sunglasses, complemented by the "I Like Ike" corsage and nylon stockings proclaiming to the world on both calves, "I Like Ike!" And what fashionable Republican woman would venture forth without her "I Like Ike" compact, in the configuration of a telephone dial, and her G.O.P. perfume, "The Scent of Victory"?[8]

As the 1950s political climate was increasingly shaped by the emergence of the Cold War and anticommunist rhetoric, the American family became a symbol of the goodness of capitalism and democracy. The more the menace of "Godless Communism" and the threat of nuclear war with the Soviet Union alarmed the public (recall the chilling "Duck and Cover" drills practiced in schools to "save" children from atomic attack), the more the themes of family and religion were combined and emphasized as antidotes. Religion — not

This pamphlet circulated by the Republican Party shows the use of family as a campaign issue. Mamie and Pat figured prominently in the strategy to present the strong American family as a deterrent to "Godless Communism."

a denominational variety — was the rather bland and amorphous "church of your choice." But family and religion continued to be used as a counter to the communist threat.[9]

The Republicans continued to capitalize on both themes: Ike and Dick were presented as religious, God-fearing, family men, while Democratic opponent Adlai Stevenson was a Unitarian. (Wasn't that something like an atheist?) The Republicans circulated campaign fliers entitled, "Ike and Dick, All American Partners," with prominent photos of Mamie and Pat. "This is the man, this is his family," read a captioned photo of Ike with Mamie looking at him adoringly. Another campaign advertisement urged, "For you, your family, your future — vote Republican." The Republican candidates and their wives seemed wholesome and traditional, appealing to postwar needs for personal and national security.[10]

In addition, the Republicans had other advantages. In Eisenhower and Nixon they had the perfect candidates for the times. Ike and Dick, as they were often called, could be presented as the warrior hero, defender of the free world against its military foes, and his running mate, the man who had built a reputation for defending the country against the subversion of Communism from within. Republicans also had the perfect presidential and vice presidential spouses, presented as the quintessentially supportive helpmates that the era extolled. Both families were active and highly visible during the campaign. This allowed Republicans to exploit skillfully the themes of the campaign, making the opposition appear weak on issues central to the fight, while highlighting the family strength and solidarity of their own candidates." Nixon even wrapped himself in family sanctity and sympathy in the dramatic "Checkers" television speech as a way to refute politically motivated charges that he misused campaign funds.

Democratic nominee, Adlai Stevenson, on the other hand, was divorced, which was itself a political liability in the fifties. Perhaps more significant, however, his marital status deprived the Democrats of the opportunity to capitalize on issues surrounding the family, a major theme of both the 1952 and 1956 campaigns.

The Democratic Party was less adept at using those

themes to appeal to women voters. Despite the decision to sponsor a ladies' day at the convention in 1952, the party's Women's Division seems not to have undertaken a voting appeal to women comparable to that mounted by the Republicans. Indeed, the Democrats produced surprisingly little campaign material of any kind for the 1952 election when compared with the Republicans' tremendous output. Instead, the party stressed the integration of women into the political mainstream and, unlike the 1948 campaign, chose not to highlight women's issues as separate from those of interest to men.[12] In 1956, the cover of the program for the Democratic National Convention featured the photograph of a happy family, but little else was done to highlight an appeal to women.

The Republicans took political campaigning with a woman's slant a step beyond domestic objects, wearing apparel, and the family. Three major Republican themes were: the Korean War; corruption in government (or "the mess in Washington," as it was called); and a balanced budget. The Republicans cleverly managed to find a particularly feminine angle for each of them. The Korean War was pictured as involving a son, husband, or boyfriend. A campaign comic book published by the Republican National Committee graphically portrayed a woman whose son was being shot at in Korea and a sweetheart whose boyfriend would be unable to make it to their wedding because the war had intervened. Ike had promised to end the war and bring the boys home. Women were told that since Ike was a brilliant military leader and knew firsthand the horrors of war, he had not only the know-how but the incentive to make peace a reality. Women obviously believed the advertising. According to pollster Louis Harris, "Women... were more disturbed about the Korean War than men in 1952. In fact, there is evidence to indicate that women were among the real prime movers in making the Korean War a major and decisive influence in the final outcome of the election."[13]

The problem of the balanced budget was also translated into the language of the average housewife — it was equated with her balancing of the family budget. The implication was clear. If SHE could do it, so could the government. A brochure displaying a housewife on the cover asked women, "How much did your groceries cost you today?" It explained the rise in prices and the high cost of living by declaring that "waste, corruption, extravagance, blunders, bungling, bureaucrats, and taxes are hidden in your grocery bag." Following the theme to its logical conclusion, Republicans circulated extra-large "Ike and Dick" shopping bags, no doubt to show the housewife just how much more she could purchase if Ike were elected.[14]

The mess in Washington was translated from an unintelligible bureaucratic problem into a simple matter that housewives could readily understand. Cleaning up the mess in Washington was portrayed in terms of a housewife cleaning up her home. Red, white, and blue scrub pails with the slogan "Let's clean up with Eisenhower and Nixon" and large "Ike and Dick" brooms, as well as broom pins, were widely distributed. Women were urged to help Ike, "a thrifty housekeeper," to "sweep out the mess."[15] Eisenhower, himself, in public and television appearances made references to "My Mamie tells me..." and proceeded to delight audiences with tales of Mamie's concern about the high cost of groceries and the mess in Washington.[15]

Pollster Louis Harris pointed out that this appeal was by no means lost on women voters. Pressures on the family budget to buy more than there was money for fell largely on women. "This was a crucial fact in the 1952 elections. Women lost faith in the Democratic Party to help them financially. Polls show... women thought there was more likelihood of the Republicans keeping prices in line than the Democrats... Women more significantly than men felt the Republican Party would bring them economic security."[16]

The Republican effort to capture the women's vote in 1952 was not without results at the polls. Earl Kruschke, after conducting polls in Michigan and studying polls of others in the 1952 election, concluded that women voted for Eisenhower in greater percentages than men (52 percent of men and 58 percent of women) and contributed significantly to his victory. Harris substantially agreed. In Kruschke's samplings, all the women interviewed who voted for Eisenhower mentioned one of the three "women's appeals" as their reason for voting Republican.[17]

Republican advisors and analysts, true to their capitalist ideology, drew heavily from their market research and advertising backgrounds to formulate the approach to the campaign. They were able to translate the issues that the Women's Division wanted to emphasize into mass-produced and mass-marketed commodities for consumption. What better way to appeal to the housewife, who was being urged back into her role as consumer? In such a climate the issues of the fifties could be sold to the electorate in female-defined terms.

Republican pamphlets and leaflets were widely circulated by the Women's Division for women party workers. One leaflet urged women to "Be A Party Girl," a double entendre that encouraged them to work for the party while, at the same time, capturing the mindless, unthreatening, "fun-time girl" of the fifties.[18] The "Party Girl" was depicted as fit for kitchen and bedroom, probably smart enough to stuff envelopes and dial phones, and certainly incapable of independent thought. Properly reticent and unassertive, she had to be taught and urged to do everything. Republican literature consistently pictured (literally) women in supportive roles, in submissive postures, receiving explicitly detailed instructions handed down to her from men or from the party on every subject. Pamphlets urged women party workers to hold telephoning, radio, and television parties. And women responded. The strength of women's political organizations at the grass-roots level was startling.[19]

The Republicans made effective use of these ardent amateurs, the local women precinct workers, who were the largest group of women in political activity at the time. These women, who then outnumbered men in political volunteer work, staged political get togethers, telephoning parties, and television sessions. The Republicans knew their constituency, depicting the American family as typically middle or upper-middle class, white, suburban, with a husband working outside the home for wages and a wife who remained at home with plenty of time for the PTA and volunteer work. Women's so-called "flexible domestic schedule" meant they had time for phoning, canvassing, meetings, tea parties, driving voters to the polls, and staffing the polls themselves.[20]

Mamie Eisenhower thoroughly enjoyed the role of political campaigner that she was thrust into and left her personal stamp on her husband's campaigns. Relatively unknown at the start of the 1952 campaign, Mamie had become a national celebrity by election time. In this first nationally televised campaign, she was an important image. A public that craved stability after World War II could not have asked for better symbols than Mamie Eisenhower and Pat Nixon to emphasize the traditional home and family. The candidates' apparent devotion to their families was reflected in their wives' adoring regard, Mamie's admiring and supportive looks at Ike during televised interviews and Pat Nixon's campaign photographs with her husband, daughters, and pet dog, Checkers.

Mamie also accompanied Ike on his whistle-stop campaign trains touring the country. At campaign stops she received local politicians and granted journalists brief interviews that introduced her to the public. Her name and likeness often appeared in women's magazines. Cries of "We want Mamie" became a familiar refrain along the Eisenhower campaign trail. At the close of his remarks Ike would announce to the audience, "And now I want you to meet my Mamie!" She was always a solid hit with the public. Photos of Ike and Mamie (both in bathrobes) on the back of the whistle-stop train became campaign classics.[21]

Never again would presidential campaigns be the same. Since that time, no presidential contender has run for office without having his wife play a significant role in the campaign. So powerful was the combination of Mamie Eisenhower's appealing presence and endearing personality with strong Republican campaign appeals to women voters, that it altered forever the political landscape and institutionalized the first lady's role as campaigner.

1. Edith P. Mayo and Denise D. Meringolo, *First Ladies: Political Role and Public Image* (Washington: The Smithsonian Institution, 1994) pp. 37-43; 65-66.
2. Earl Roger Kruschke, *The Woman Voter*. (Washington: Public Affairs Press, 1955), p. 4.
3. For information on the formation and work of the Democratic and Republican Parties' Women's Divisions see: *Republican Women are Wonderful: A History of Women at Republican National Conventions.* (Washington: National Women's Political Caucus, 1980); *Democratic Women are Wonderful: A History of Women at Democratic National Conventions.* (Washington: National Women's Political Caucus, 1980); and Susan Ware, *Partner and I: Molly Dewson, Feminism, and New Deal Politics.* (New Haven: Yale Univ. Press, 1987).
4. Advertising giants such as Rosser Reeves and Madison Avenue's Batton, Barton, Durstine and Osborn (BBDO) played major roles in the Eisenhower campaign. See William L. Bird, Jr., "TV and the Ike Age," in Keith Melder, *Hail to the Candidate: Presidential Campaigns From Banners to Broadcasts.* (Washington: Smithsonian Institution, 1992), pp. 161-174.
5. Charles McGovern, *Sold American: Inventing the Consumer 1890-1940.* (Ph.D. Dissertation, Harvard Univ., 1993), Chapter II, esp. Section B, "Courting Mrs. Consumer: Women and Advertisers, 1890-1930" and Chapter III.
6. Edith Mayo, "Be a Party Girl: Campaign Appeals to Women," in Melder, *Hail to the Candidate*, pp. 149-151; Melder, *Hail to the Candidate*; Louise M. Young, "Women's Place in American Politics: The Historical Perspective," *Journal of Politics 38* (August 1976); Mary P. Ryan, *Women in Public: From Banners to Ballots, 1825-1880.* (Baltimore: Johns Hopkins Univ. Press, 1990); Paula Baker, "The Domestication of American Politics: Women and American Political Society, 1780-1920," *American Historical Review 89* (June 1984); and Roger A. Fischer, *Tippecanoe and Trinkets Too: The Material Culture of American Presidential Campaigns, 1828-1984.* (Urbana: Univ. of Illinois Press, 1988).
7. Mayo and Meringolo, *First Ladies*, pp. 41-43.

8. These material culture objects of the campaigns are housed in the Division of Social History's Political Collections, National Museum of American History (NMAH), Smithsonian Institution. Similar objects can be found in the H. Doyle DeWitt Collection at the Univ. of Hartford, Hartford, Connecticut, and in private collections. See: Mayo, "Be a Party Girl," in Melder, *Hail to the Candidate,* p. 154.

9. *Ibid.,* pp. 156-157.

10. *Ibid.,* p. 157.

11. *Ibid.,* p. 152.

12. *Ibid.*

13. Louis Harris, *Is There a Republican Majority?: Political Trends 1952-1956.* (New York: Harper and Bros., 1954), p. 111 (quotation) and Chapter 7; also Sandra Baxter and Marjorie Lansing, *Women and Politics: The Visible Majority.* (Ann Arbor: The Univ. of Michigan Press, 1983). These women discuss the voting patterns of women historically, including the 1952 election, and examine the growing gender gap in electoral politics in the past decade and its potential effects.

14. Mayo, "Be a Party Girl," p. 156; The brochure, "How Much Did Your Groceries Cost Today?" was published in Washington by the Republican National Committee, 1952. It can be located in the Smithsonian's NMAH, Political Collections.

15. *Ibid.*

16. Harris, *Is There a Republican Majority?* p. 110.

17. Kruschke, *Woman Voter,* p. 4, 6-14. Also Harris, *Is There a Republican Majority?* Chapter 7.

18. Mayo, "Be a Party Girl," p. 153.

19. "Political Pilgrim's Progress —Women Organize for Action," *Ladies Home Journal* 69 (September 1952), pp. 25, 162. This article outlined political activity of both Republican and Democratic Women's Divisions and gave a view of how vast this network had become in the fifties. See also: Marion K. Sanders, *The Lady and the Vote* (Boston: Houghton Mifflin, 1956).

20. Mayo, "Be a Party Girl," p. 153-154.

21. *Ibid.*

Mamie's Hats: The White House, the New Look, and the Meaning of Style in the 1950s

Dr. Karal Ann Marling

I n 1952, shortly after the GOP convention, Norman Rockwell went to Denver to paint Ike for the cover of the *Saturday Evening Post*. They met in an 8th floor suite at the Brown Palace Hotel. The time was short. Rockwell had two hours before the General was scheduled to leave on a much needed fishing vacation. Rockwell tried for the famous Ike grin first — and got only smiling lips until he mentioned grandchildren. Then the smile became real. He tried a military pose of command, too steely, as it turned out, for the *Post* cover. He did a sketch of Mamie after Ike left. But even when the two men were alone in the suite, swapping recipes for tomato soup and tips on painting, Rockwell recalled, Mrs. Eisenhower seemed to be there. "{The General} had spoken of Mrs. Eisenhower several times as if she were in the room," the artist wrote. "She seemed always close at hand in his thinking, affectionately complementing him as he struggled his way through the searing life that has come to him, and he complementing her. Mamie had told her husband not to make faces that showed the gold fillings in his teeth and Ike meekly obeyed."

The story is a charming one and there seems little doubt in retrospect that Rockwell's happy image of Dwight Eisenhower helped to elect a man who could also look formidable enough to terrify whole armies. Style has political and social implications. The relaxed, domesticated Ike — Rockwell's perpetually grinning Grandpa — became the President. Although Americans respected the man for the generalship reflected in Rockwell's other sketches, the happy Eisenhower suited the emotional mood and needs of the 1950s. You could call it Ike's "New Look." The real "New Look," of course, was a style of women's fashion created by Paris designer Christian Dior in 1947. After seven long years of wartime make-do, rationing, and stringent rules governing the amount of fabric permissible in a given garment, after seven years of skimpy, asexual suits and silence from the great French couturiers, fashion and femininity were back at last. Dior's suits were sensuous, positively luxurious — gloriously full in the skirt, and topped off with great, extravagant cartwheel hats. Nipped at the waist, rounded at the hips and bustline, sloping gracefully through the shoulder, they defined the body's every womanly, viva la difference contour. The silhouette was so different, so utterly novel and wonderful that *Life* magazine christened it "The New Look." La guerre est fini!

But the New Look has never really stopped being controversial. Fashion experts still squabble over Dior's authorship of the style. Weren't Scarlett O'Haras laced corsets and crinolines in the 1939 movie, *Gone With the Wind*, as "new look" as anything turned out by the House of Dior?

Others, less concerned with issues of primacy and more interested in meaning, recoil from what designer and fashion photographer Cecil Beaton called the "wanton fantasy" of the New Look — an artificial, manufactured woman whose anatomical differences were exaggerated to conform to the sexual dimorphism of the 40s and 50s. Was a woman who stuffed herself into a girdle and high heels a woman at all, by the hard-body, in-your- face standards of the 1990s? Wasn't she some form of sexual chattel? A piece of pretty, consumer-culture, top-of-the-T.V.-set bric-a-brac?

She was, without question, artful, and the harbinger of what one design specialist dubs "A radical shift in aesthetic" which would, by the middle of the 1950s, transform everything from bric-a-brac and automobiles to cakes, plastic cups and saucers, high-style furniture, and off-the-rack, department store outfits. The postwar aesthetic asserted the importance of deliberate artfulness, of close attention to matters of color, line, and form.

One strain of 50s design was organic — a synonym for curvilinear, volumetric, vaguely bosomy shapes: the New Look was organic to a fault but so was the tumescence on the back fender of the Cadillac (1948-ca.l953) that would shortly become a fullfledged tail fin. A second strain was two-dimensional, textural and richly patterned, like a vintage Pollock. It was colorful, obtrusive, and lavish. A little too much, perhaps. Like yards of figured peau de soie with dyed-to-match gloves and shoes.

In the most fundamental of ways, the New Look is about looking, too — about distinctive forms, eye-catching patterns and textures, and attractive colors; about looking at people and their clothes and being looked at in turn; about thinking about looking. Looking: not the judgmental "gaze" of contemporary feminist theory, perhaps, but something more like a scrupulous, pleasurable regard for both shape and surface. In this respect, there is something post-literate about the 50s. And the association of a diagnostic habit of vision with sensual enjoyment makes the New Look all the harder to talk about. Or rather, it is all too easy to dismiss as trivial and superficial the lives of those who looked for their own reflections in the era's glittering surfaces.

Applied to the female body, the principles of the New Look exuded a palpable optimism. If its basic shape could be changed, so could the human condition or, at the very least, the life of the lady in the son-of-Dior suit. Things were always perfectible, just as form — one's own included — was invariably improved by the complex play of pattern against contour and volume. So the old rules of finality no longer pertained. In the design ethos of the New Look, everything was always brand, spanking new.

Because externals are the usual bases of advertising, the notion that style and appearances may actually matter is distressing to many critics of American mass culture weaned on Vance Packard's 1957 expose of Madison Avenue. Frederic Jameson traces the beginnings of the post-modern malaise to the point just after World War II when the empty blandishments of advertising accelerated the already "rapid rhythm of fashion and styling changes." By virtue of its intimate proximity with the body, however, fashion also functions as an extension of personality, a medium through which autobiographical statements (true or false ones) are made manifest. "Clothes are a sort of theatre where the leading player — the self— is torn between functions and decoration, protection and assertion, concealment and display," posits British design critic Stephen Bayley. In fitting rooms all across America, women twirling before mirrors in their first New Look skirts understood the dynamic perfectly. Pretty clothes not only enhanced the self; the theater of fashion also allowed the wearer to explore multiple identities and potential starring roles. In her satiric memoir of suburban life in the 1950s, Margaret Halsey described a shopping excursion to the city that changed a dutiful housewife into a sex goddess the moment she tried on "a silk print which, worn with very high heels and my hair in a French roll, makes me look properly carnal..., as if I had my mind on lower things." Ironically, the mass-produced New Look uniform of the 50s invited the shopper to try on a new persona, primal and highly individualized — a self usually hidden from the public gaze by skirts and hats and little silk prints.

Clothing manufacturers and marketers were sensitive to the intrinsic theatricality of fashion and its dual capacity to influence the perceptions of both audience and actress. The first in a long and famous series of theater-of-the-absurd lingerie ads, released in October of 1949, pictured a woman mysteriously out and about at the local supermarket clad only in a New Look skirt (with coordinating purse and beads) and a brassiere. "I dreamed I went shopping in my Maidenform bra," the copy announced. The highly successful Maidenform campaign drew on suburbanized Surrealism and popularized Freud to glamorize the underpinnings demanded by the new style: the model's "dream" discloses suppressed yearnings of a distinctly genteel sort — to shop, to be an artist, a lady editor, a fashion designer, a grande dame bound for the opera with a neckful of jewels and a mink stole. Nevertheless, her state of demi-nudity establishes the missing costume as the link between a private, interior life of repressed desires and the public world of action, from which unclothed persons are firmly barred. By the absence thereof, Maidenform ads speak to the intricacies and pleasures of fashion, and its importance as a

31

signifier of meaning. And in the heyday of the New Look, the refrain of the nocturnal dreamer with nothing to wear became a national watchword. The press was properly delighted one day early in her husband's first term, therefore, when Mamie Eisenhower — an unrepentant clothes-horse — dropped in backstage at a Washington fashion show. Quipped a flustered model, caught in her underwear by the First Lady: "Gosh, I never dreamt I'd meet Mrs. Eisenhower in my Maidenform bra!"

As her choice of a White House wardrobe demonstrated, Mrs. Eisenhower was a passionate but prudent devotee of the New Look throughout the 1950s, preferring the less extreme American adaptations of Dior's original concept. She was an early convert, too, quick to equate the "New" with a youthfulness of attitude she cultivated and freely discussed. To be young meant trying the latest thing. And whether that novelty was the packaged cake mix with which she stocked the family pantry at 1600 Pennsylvania Avenue, the "1950s modern" furniture with which she redecorated the presidential retreat at Camp David, or the new T.V. soap operas which she adored (*As the World Turns* was her hands-down favorite), Mamie Eisenhower was determined to give it a whirl.

In 1948, years before the General decided to run for public office, the *Brownsville Herald* interviewed "Ike's wife" about her taste in clothes. The reporter found her looking much younger than her 51 years and partial to unmatronly fashions. "Hats don't interest her particularly," the writer noted, "but she loves shoes. She likes the longer dresses of the 'new look' but hopes they don't get too close to the ankles." She liked fitted bodices, sweetheart necklines, and flirty skirts that swished when she walked — an ultra-feminine version of Dior filtered through Hollywood — and wore them for the next decade, when a grandmother of more sedate disposition might have settled into Mother Hubbards. Since she was constantly in the public eye and known for her delight in her well-stocked closets, Mrs. Eisenhower became both an exemplar of the new fashion sensibility of her day and an example of the precise terms in which the New Look appealed to postwar America.

In 1950, President Truman sent Ike to Europe to head

NATO. Mamie joined him in 1951, emerging as a newsworthy figure in her own right for the first time, partly because of fashion. French journalists were intrigued by the likes and dislikes of a lady from exotic Iowa, while women's pages back home wondered how one of their number would fare in the dazzling world of haute couture. The powerful mystique of the dress salon was explored in a spate of fashion movies beginning with the 1952 *Lovely to Look At*, starring Kathryn Grayson as part-owner of a struggling Paris design establishment. What these films have in common is an aura of exclusivity and wealth (French fashion is for the rich), a sense of womanly competence, and an emphasis on headgear. In the Hollywood version of the fashion business, the salon is a place in which men are tolerated for the sake of romantic duets or financial expertise. But it is a woman's place, ultimately governed by her preferences and skills. The hat is a badge of membership in the sisterhood of the empowered: fashion commentators and editors, poker-faced mannequins, salesgirls, brisk premieres, designers, and knowing customers all wear outrageous confections atop their carefully coiffed heads.

It should come as no surprise, then, that Mamie Eisenhower discovered hats in Paris. Thereafter, she wore a hat to complete a costume, to signify a public appearance or a special occasion, to announce her kinship with other hatted ladies who ran the charity functions she attended. The hat was a luxury item as well, too small and delicate to shield the head from the elements, but visually obtrusive and subject to radical seasonal change, a prime example of what Packard meant by a "status symbol." Yet, in America's vibrant new consumer culture, luxuries once reserved for the rich were within reach of everybody. When asked about a stunning new hat she wore to a state affair in Paris, Mamie replied: "I got it by mail order from home. It cost me $9.95!" Much to the chagrin of the French press, she then launched into a gleeful account of rummaging through the racks at department stores for high fashion bargains. Mamie, it seems, had no interest in one-of-a-kind New Look clothes when the same thing could be had for a song in Macy's or Bloomingdale's. She attended the Paris shows regularly but never bought a thing. "Can you see my paying seven

The Eisenhowers at Washington, D.C. airport, c. 1952.
(Dwight D. Eisenhower Library)

hundred dollars for a dress?" she asked a visiting columnist from the States.

Once ensconced in the White House, Mamie's rummaging days were over. She drew mobs whenever her gleaming black Chrysler pulled up to a store and sale-rack frugality was politically inexpedient besides. "We had a hard time convincing her that she couldn't wear two-year-old dresses," said Mollie Parnis, her favorite American designer. "I told her, 'It's like [an old] Cadillac around Washington. You just can't do it. It would be bad for our industry.'" During the 1952 campaign, however, there were no such constraints on her fashion instincts. She wore her mail-order hats (and a couple of numbers bought in Paris). And she made excellent copy by being most emphatic about her personal fashion dos and don'ts.

Photographed for a biography in *Collier's* wearing a sleeveless, halter-top sundress with a billowing skirt that "made her look more like a girl than a mature woman," Mrs. Eisenhower made it clear that she had chosen her wild cotton print deliberately: "I hate old-lady clothes. And I shall never wear them." As much as a friendly smile and an ease of manner, her insistence on young lines and cuts — after all, teenagers were wearing big felt skirts decorated with poodle dogs in 1951 and 1952 — may have encouraged the public to call her "Mamie." At any rate, during the Eisenhowers' whistlestop tour of the nation, her sense of style soon became familiar to anybody who followed the campaign in the media. *Newsweek* scooped its rivals by tracing six of the outfits to the 7th Avenue salesrooms of Mollie Parnis in New York City. Mamie liked Parnis's clothes, she confessed, because they had bouffant skirts and that "little extra flair."

Letters to the designer from the campaign trail date the beginning of their long relationship to the early summer of 1952 and Mamie's purchase of a navy blue silk shantung Parnis dress at Bonwit Teller. The dress had acquired a prominent spot somewhere around Chicago, possibly as the result of water leaking from a bouquet of flowers presented by the party faithful. Mamie complained — and promptly ordered five more dresses and a faille suit which caught up with the entourage in Minnesota on an October day too cold for any of the new finery. In late November, with the election won, Parnis and Eisenhower were engrossed in fittings for a Washington wardrobe. In December, Parnis found herself on the official guest list for the forthcoming inauguration ceremonies. At Christmas, she sent her client a bright red taffeta dress for a gift. "What a perfectly beautiful...dress," wrote Mamie gratefully, "and in a style that is so becoming to me, too!"

The style Mamie found most becoming was a one-piece dress (sometimes a suit) with a full skirt and a thirteen-inch hemline, usually made up in a fabric with a reflective or slightly iridescent surface-like silk taffeta. The dress itself was a fancy, ornamental variation on the shirtwaist, the relaxed, suburban edition of the New Look seen everywhere from shopping centers to junior high schools in the American ginghams introduced in the spring of 1950. It was a "lady look": neat, coherent, feminine, and yet, without the more extreme forms of corsetry and built-in structure, one which permitted a freedom of movement in keeping with car pools, servantless homes, and the other conventions of modern housewifery. Mollie Parnis did not admit to any interest in "designing for the average housewife," but the Parnis dress did stake out a middle ground between Paris and Levittown. Her firm, wrote one fashion historian, "produced flattering dresses...for the well-to-do woman over thirty, emphasizing becomingness in beautiful fabrics [and] a conservative interpretation of current trends."

Unlike high fashion clothes, the Parnis shirtwaist made a woman look well turned out but *normal*, a term the designer also used to describe her most famous client in the mid-1950s. "That is the nicest thing about her," Mollie Parnis gushed. "She's making maturity glamorous." In later years, Parnis could be cruel in her criticisms of Mrs. Eisenhower, claiming that she had been forced to accessorize Mamie s outfits, lest the First Lady commit some awful error of taste: "You know, she really didn't have much fashion sense." Other members of the design profession also sniffed at Mamie's relish for dyed-to-match shoes and colored stockings, mink coats, charm bracelets, and bangs. In the end, however, what she called "looking high class" — adorning a basic style with marks of familial success and

individuality — came to be known as "the Mamie look."
Subordinating dress to ensemble and ensemble to
personality, it was not a look calculated to advertise a
designers product: the ultimate Mamie-ness of a given outfit
all but overshadowed the contribution of a Mollie Parnis or a
Nettie Rosenstein. And when she decided that she looked
"high class," even the contrary opinions of the experts fazed
her not at all. Dior raised hems in the spring of 1953 but
Mamie didn't. *Life* magazine made fun of her hairstyle but
she ignored suggestions for a change so studiously that
bangs became a key element of "the Mamie look."

The public was fascinated by the sheer distinctiveness of
her perky forelock: while fashion trends seemed calculated
to turn women into so many mass-produced robots in
pseudo-Diors, Mamie Eisenhower's hairdo called attention
to itself by its sheer oddity. Hollywood columnist Hedda
Hopper facetiously asked whether, if she became First Lady,
Mamie would expect all the women in America to wear
bangs. A week after the election, *Life* demanded that she
trim the bangs and get a poodle cut instead, and provided
retouched pictures to prove that with one, simple change,
she could be "the best looking first lady we have ever had."

But as hairdressers were quick to point out, the poodle cut
was an unforgiving style, too, because the hair was curled
away from the face, exposing every sag and wrinkle. It was a
young look best suited to the young complexion of an
authentic gamin whereas the customers who filled
Washington's beauty salons on the eve of the inauguration,
demanding "The Mamie," wanted instead the youthful
illusion the wife of the President-elect so buoyantly
projected. The adventurous among them got a haircut. The
timid settled for false bangs priced from $10 to $17.50. The
"Mamie look" of the early 50s had an additive quality: bangs
appended to the hairline, gauntlet gloves pulled up over
dress sleeves, ditzy hats atop an elaborate hairdo (Elizabeth
Arden even provided a diagram to insure complete
uniformity in cut and set), and a mink tossed over
everything.

The effect was busy and acquisitive, somehow, as if each
layer — brooch on bodice under coat; hat plus hair plus
lipstick and earrings — were too important in its own right

to subside quietly into some fashion ensemble. It was possessive, obtrusive, infinitely pleased with things that shimmered and glistened, or swished, or dangled. The noisy, hopelessly jejune charm bracelet was Mamie-ism in its purest form. Most photos of Mrs. Eisenhower campaigning with her husband show her posing so as to call attention to a lucky "Ike" charm or a huge four-leaf clover medallion. She owned several similar bracelets, including one with twenty-one charms representing important milestones in the career of her husband, made by a Fifth Avenue jeweler who specialized in expensive versions of a fad more popular among teenagers, coeds, and debutantes. But the presentation of a biographical bracelet was also a highlight of *This is Your Life*, a popular new Wednesday night television show devoted to humanizing celebrities by revealing incidents from their private lives. With the charm bracelet, life literally became a fashion statement. It was a sign of accomplishment, a proof that the good life of fame and stardom and obtrusive jewelry had been well earned.

The formal components of 1950s fashion appear in other artifacts of the decade which also expressed and enhanced the pleasures of ownership by means of accretion. 1952-model kitchen stoves didn't work better for having pushbuttons and colored trim applied to the surface; cars didn't idle more smoothly thanks to a two-tone paint job or several pounds of chrome "gorp" on the front bumper; improved reception in a radio or television set was not a function of the woven and textured finishes and the metallic highlights adorning the cabinet. Yet these superfluous details were the visual luxuries, "the little extra flair," Mamie also looked for in her clothes. They made life sparkle and glitter. They made it fun to get dressed in the morning, to cook, to drive. The extras were the bright lights, the music, the glamour, the excitement, the pizzazz, the gleaming charms.

Fur was the ultimate 1950s extra. By the time of the 1952 elections, the ranch mink coat had also acquired partisan connotations. A year earlier, a congressional committee investigating corruption in the Truman administration turned up evidence of bribery in the form of a $9,540 pastel mink hanging in the closet of a White House stenographer.

The televised "Checkers" speech, in which Eisenhower's running mate, Richard Nixon, attempted to clear himself of charges that he had tapped a secret slush fund, exploited that symbol of decadent luxury shamelessly. His wife, Pat, didn't own a mink coat, the candidate boasted: "But she does have a respectable Republican cloth coat, and I always tell her that she would look good in anything." There matters rested until Mamie waded in on the side of fashion. On December 1, wearing what seemed to be a full-length mink, she turned up to accompany the departing First Lady on the traditional tour of the Executive Mansion. As the women posed for pictures at the door (Bess Truman in a modest Persian lamb topper), reporters eyed the glossy Republican fur and needled Mrs. Eisenhower about it, trying to get a newsworthy quote. What was her coat made of, anyway? "Mink, of course," shot back Mrs. Eisenhower with a broad smile and a winning tinkle of her charm bracelet. Politics had nothing to do with nice clothes. Didn't *everybody* want a mink coat? Or the next best thing — a mink stole?

Her fur labeled Mamie a winner, a success. Democrat, Republican: those were dim abstractions. Fur was real and so was Mamie's transparent joy in finding herself under the White House portico equipped with all the sartorial trappings of the American Dream: a pearl choker; a drop-dead mink pulled back to reveal a Mollie Parnis shirtwaist with pleats, a ruffle, and covered buttons; matching Cuban-heel pumps; a big, shiny alligator purse; and a little velvet hat. Texture, color, complexity, contrast: dressed to kill, she was a walking compendium of the aesthetic principles that governed the marketplace. And for that reason, she managed to look very much like the woman next door. The velvet hat was by Sally Victor, who told the *New York Times* that Mamie exemplified "good American taste."

Sally Victor began her career in the 1930s as a protege of Dorothy Saver, the influential Lord and Taylor vice president who promoted American fashion in the Fifth Avenue windows of the store. The American quality Victor prized in fashion was a kind of purposeful playfulness best expressed in millinery. Specifically, she thought of hats in psychological terms, as disguises, indices of character, mirrors of mood, or means of trying on new aspects of a complex personality. "A woman becomes what her hat means to the world and to herself," the milliner wrote. Fighting the postwar drift toward a more casual, hatless lifestyle — despite the pictures in fashion magazines, younger women and teens owned far fewer hats than their elders — Victor stayed at the top of her profession in the 1950s by conceding the avant-garde end of the trade to Mr. John and to her arch-rival, Lily Dace. The "Sally V" subsidiary, which accounted for half of her business, produced hats for the mass market, priced within the reach of most bareheaded suburbanites. They sold briskly because Victor emphasized the concept of prettiness: "All you have to do" to sell hats, she counseled, "is show a woman that she looks prettier with a hat on than off."

Pretty was not chic, of course. Whereas chic required external verification, pretty was an entirely more comfortable concept, grounded in how a woman felt about herself. "Good fashion is an individual matter," Victor asserted. "It is whatever makes you look better. I do not believe in any style that does not make the wearer prettier." Prettiness was ageless, besides. Pretty girls were like melodies; children called their mothers "pretty"; women used the term to describe one another, or a new hat. Meeting Pat Nixon for the first time at the Republican convention in Chicago, Mamie Eisenhower turned to her and blurted out, "Why, you're the prettiest thing!" "The little flowered one is just as pretty as it can be and terribly sweet," she told Sally Victor after her 1953 Easter bonnet arrived at the White House. And if Mrs. Eisenhower worried that another woman was feeling unpretty and ill at ease, her folk remedy was always a new hat. She ordered four Sally V's —"Young hats — she's so pretty!"— as a gift for Elizabeth of England when the Queen paid a state visit in 1957 dressed in matronly British woolens, and another in 1959 for the dowdy Nina Khrushchev, who didn't dare wear such a blatant emblem of capitalist excess in public.

Mamie's most celebrated hat, the "airwave" model, was the one she wore to her husband's 1953 swearing-in and to the massive inaugural parade that followed. It was a Sally Victor, of course. Shaped like a shallow, inverted bowl or an iced cupcake, the hat was made of soft gray felt, contoured into four scalloped layers and slashed to show flashes of a bright green lining. Because the festivities were covered at length on television, Mamie's costume came in for unprecedented scrutiny. Her gray Hattie Carnegie dressmaker suit was hidden under her mink, and her charm bracelet peeped out of her sleeve only when she waved, but the cheerful little hat was hard to miss, especially in "human interest" shots of the First Lady slipping off a shoe and bending over to massage an aching arch as the parade dragged on toward nightfall.

Macy's sold knock-offs by the gross. Of the seven hundred letters per week directed to Mrs. Eisenhower by the general public in the following weeks, many asked for that hat, or one just like it. Mamie's letter to Sally Victor — one of the first pieces of post-inaugural business to be attended to — proved the latter's point about psychology and headgear. "All your hats were beautiful and styled so becomingly," she wrote, "but I think the one that attracted the most comment and admiration was the soft gray hat with the lovely green lining peeking through. An attractive, flattering hat always helps me feel my best and look my most confident, so you can see your selections were so important in boosting my morale."

The other components of her Washington wardrobe paled into insignificance beside the all-important inaugural ballgown, however. Stories circulated about the special plywood crate built to convey the dress to Washington, about the three hours it took to dispose the built-in petticoats properly, as the President ("By golly, Mamie, you're beautiful!") paced the floor in a fit of impatience. Magazines ran inch by inch descriptions of the gown. Mamie dolls and figurines were garbed in Renoir pink peau de soie dresses with matching above-the-elbow gloves, shoes, and evening bags. Like the gray suit, the dress and all its accessories were ordered through Neiman-Marcus of Dallas. Lawrence Marcus selected the designers and commissioned the clothes but in the case of her gown, Mrs. Eisenhower personally specified a wide skirt, chose the color, and insisted that Nettie Rosenstein supply additional glitter in the form of 2,000 hand-sewn rhinestones in four sizes and several variegated shades of pink. Concentrated in the gathers just below the dropped waistline, where the gown was at its fullest, the stones drew attention to the lavish use of material and to feminine curves already exaggerated by stiff taffeta underskirts. It was a New Look extravaganza, embellished and enriched American style.

In stylistic terms, the ballgown anticipated most of the ingredients of vintage Mamie-ism. All the designers who made clothes for Mrs. Eisenhower during her White House years — Parnis, Carnegie, Elizabeth Arden's fashion division — would use some variation on the bouffant skirt with added fullness at the sides, most often placing bunches of unpressed pleats like paniers over each hipbone or achieving the same effect with peplum jackets. Gathered into narrow twists of silk at the shoulder, the gown exposed what *Life* called her "pretty neck and shoulders:" the shoulder would be soft, unseamed, and natural in her daytime outfits, too. And her street clothes would be decorated, the basic structure already enhanced with unusual or non-functional buttons, cording, false pockets, and plackets before she began to add jewelry and accessories on her own initiative. The inaugural extras — faux pearls and brilliants by Trifari, an evening bag encrusted with pink stones and beads — matched the gown but were in no way subordinated to it: the things Mrs. Eisenhower carried or pinned to her everyday dresses would remain equally distinct, as if to call attention to the fact that they were hers and that she alone had decided to wear them. This was an American style, a newer, showier, happier, shop-'til-you-drop New Look. It was everything that haute couture was not; pretty, busy, flouncy, clothes-proud, quirkily personal, oblivious of age, all decked out, studied but still a little slapdash. Garnished like a colorful Jell-O salad. After details of the ballgown hit the papers, the New York Dress Institute named Mamie to its list of the world's twelve best-dressed women.

She made the lists every year. Best-dressed (along with the Duchess of Windsor, Mrs. William Paley, and other high-priestesses of fashion orthodoxy). Best-hatted. Best-shod. Her shopping trips, and every item purchased, were considered newsworthy. So was the story of Mamie and a lobbyist's wife arriving at a diplomatic reception in virtually the same Mollie Parnis. As the offending party retreated into a distant room clutching her mink cape over the blue and green print — "Don't hide it," cried Mamie. "I think its pretty!" — Parnis explained that many of Mrs. Eisenhower's "originals" were off-the-rack models with fuller skirts and special trim. Anybody could dress just like she did and manufacturers counted on Mamie's down-to-earth taste to revive the retail end of the business. "She is as likely to buy a dress she likes for $50 as she is to order an exclusive custom-made one," noted an economic observer. "What pleases the moguls of the nations $11 billion fashion industry is that Mrs. Eisenhower can be counted on to wear either with an air."

The best way to guarantee Mamie's presence at a charity event, the joke went, was to hold a fashion show. A typical list of engagements for a two-week period in the spring of 1953, for example, included style show benefits mounted by the Naval War College Officers' Wives Club, the Cherry Blossom Festival, and the National Symphony Orchestra. A popular form of activity for women's organizations in the 1950s, the fashion show was a highly specialized dramatic form — a ritualized pantomime of shopping, and a play in which audience and performers were equally well costumed. Indeed, model and viewer were often one and the same person, as club officers did their turns on the runway, reminding the rest of the spectators that fashion always had the dual aspect of looking and being looked at, performing and appraising.

These are not trivial matters — in terms of the GNP or in terms of understanding the values of a culture. Academic feminists have often shunned fashion — its pleasures and its significance — because their models for the proper behavior of women are men, ca. 1975 — not Mrs. Eisenhower's world, and not, I might add, our own. Historians of all sorts have neglected the artifactual record that includes hats and Trifari jewelry in favor of written records reflecting, I would suggest, the preoccupations of those who write such documents. But the language of words is by no means the only utterance of concern to the culture as a whole. Texts miss the subtlety of play, disguise, self-re-invention. In the 1950s, to be sure, Mamie Eisenhower's hats said it better.

Mamie Eisenhower: An Insight from her Personal Letters

Susan Eisenhower

You have to know what a great treat it is for me to be here in Gettysburg to see so many old friends and to be here for this special occasion, marking the 100th anniversary of my grandmother's birth. It's really an emotional experience to be here. My grandparents' death has been an end of a real era for all members of our family, and so I've had to relive some very, very important years of my life. And I did so in a marvelous way. I had the tremendous luck and opportunity to be able to learn about my grandparents' early lives through a remarkable set of correspondence that Mamie wrote to her parents between about 1907 and 1952. That is the record on which this book is based. Of course, I used many other sources. I think what emerges is an extremely different view of Mamie Eisenhower than is currently depicted. In fact, in many ways, I think they are going to have to rewrite all the chapters on Mamie in the First Ladies books. But what emerges, of course, is a much stronger, much more independent, much more emotional Mamie than we see from the kinds of accounts that are so often told.

Mamie really did have a way of being very quick. One of the most famous stories, which came out just at a time when the American public was trying to figure out whether Mamie Eisenhower would one day be First Lady, occurred during granddads posting as Chief of Staff of the Army. It was during General Marshall's retirement dinner when the emcee got up and said, "The only thing General Marshall is really looking forward to doing right now is to retire to Leesburg with Mrs. Eisenhower." He realized suddenly his mistake, and said, "Oh, my dear, my apologies to the General." To which Mamie piped up, "Which General?" This became a story that made the headlines as America was trying to figure who this woman is, this Mamie Eisenhower. We all know that she had her very special idiosyncrasies and peculiarities. That was one of the things that actually made being her granddaughter such fun. It's only now that I've been through her correspondence that I understand the significance of the fact that when you rang the doorbell at her house in the summer, invariably she would kiss you and hand you a fly swatter. Now having read the correspondence of her life in Panama and the Philippines, to say that she disliked insects would be putting it mildly. And so, one could often see guests sitting around the sun porch at the farm holding fly swatters.

In the course of my interviews, I had a wonderful opportunity to talk to Harry Butcher's daughter. She and her mother, Ruth, were living with Mamie at the Wardman Tower during World War II. She used to comment that the Butchers had a very tragic divorce after World War II and this really was one of the reasons they did not stay close to Ike and Mamie. It was largely because my Grandmother felt very strongly sympathetic to Harry Butcher's wife. In any case, Mamie, deeply loyal person that she was, stayed in touch with Ruth Butcher all of her life. Her daughter, Beverly, told me this wonderful story that Mamie would often call after seeing the soap operas. She would get on the phone and say, "Well, what are we going to wear tomorrow?" meaning, "What are we going to wear to the soap opera wedding?" So she and her mother would make little jokes like that.

In Abilene they'll tell you that Mamie liked to come in very quietly, in her widowhood, to see the grave of her husband and her son. She never told anybody that she was coming, but everybody in town knew when she was there because they would see the limousine going through the Taco Bell take-out. You can imagine Mamie, probably draped in mink, going through the Taco Bell take-out. Well, of course, her love of Tex-Mex food was connected with her many years in San Antonio.

Though she is not remembered as being a great cook, she

did master quite a number of Tex-Mex recipes. During the war, believe it or not, Bess Truman convened a group at the White House to study Spanish. Mamie was among them and she was responsible for bringing the Tex-Mex recipes. One can only imagine both how the food turned out and how much Spanish they learned.

Typical of Mamie, in all ways, she had this tremendous sympathy for the women in her life. It didn't matter how one woman's husband might get along with her own husband. She cared not the least about the men's relationships. A good example of that is the deep and close relationship she had with Jean MacArthur and also with Bess Truman. I think that was really a marvelous thing about her.

This book is based on about 300 unpublished letters. Most of them are Mamies letters to her parents, but quite a number of them are, in fact, Ike's letters to his parents-in-law which, in some respects, are every bit as revealing as her letters to her parents.

I don't know if the role the Douds played in the personal development of Dwight Eisenhower is well understood. First of all, you have to get the setting. We have a Denver family, quite wealthy, in the meat packing business. Poopah, who was my great-grandfather, and Nana, Mamie's mother, whose real name was Elvira, produced four girls. So we have a young Mamie, a debutante, from a well-to-do family, meets Dwight Eisenhower, one of seven boys, six surviving children altogether, from a family that is really impoverished in sheer monetary terms. But a very dignified, a very God-fearing family, from Kansas.

I'd like to say that this is Mars meets Venus big time. If there was ever a woman who was deeply grounded and deeply proud of her own feminine being, it was Mamie Eisenhower. And I certainly don't have to tell you about Dwight Eisenhower. As Mamie said, he was the handsomest man she ever saw. And I think that this very profound difference in their background really had a great deal to do with the life long engagement between the two of them. They had a real marriage, and I mean a real marriage in every sense of the word. It was a deeply engaged relationship. Sometimes it included irritation and impatience, but it also involved great love, affection, devotion.

And so, I'd really like to tell you a little bit about Mamie through the letters I discovered. The sort of frivolous Mamie that appears sometimes, the sort of fun Mamie, is actually a Mamie who had a very big decision to make rather early on in her life. Before she married Ike, all four of her grandparents had died. By the time she was 24 years old, every one of her grandparents was dead, both of her sisters had died, and she'd lost her first born son. In addition to that, she came from a family that took death very, very seriously. My father always thought the Douds were a little on the morose side from time to time. But after the deaths of these sisters, especially the first one, Mamie would be taken out to Fairmount Cemetery in Denver every Sunday. In the beginning they went every day to the cemetery; but after the initial shock of death had worn off, they went every Sunday. Every Sunday of her childhood, she went to the cemetery. And they each would stand there, no matter what the weather. She once told us that she could hear the cooing of doves, the wind blowing through trees in the cemetery, and she thought that this was just about the most frightening experience she ever had. Whenever she heard birds cooing, she always said it would take her back to that mournful period of time.

The Douds on the other hand, the same family that went out to the cemetery constantly, were also people who made a huge celebration of every holiday and everyone's birthday. There are some marvelous letters in here about Mamie's birthdays, and what she was going to get for her birthday. This was a kind of festival of love. In fact, a rather strange custom on birthdays was that they would start a long procession at the top of the staircase and sing "Here Comes the Bride." Figure that out. We're still wondering at our household because we don't know what the bride had to do with the birthday. But this was a great formality that took place every year at the time of one of the girls' birthdays.

I think Mamie, after the death of her second sister, understood that she had a fundamental choice to make. That she could either go through life laughing, or she could go through life crying. Certainly by the time her first son died, this was a very, very stark choice. So I would like to read to you some of the passages from the letters that I think are so moving. This is the kind of life they shielded from the public. In fact, my mother often said that the strategy was so successful that we have a kind of trivialized view of Mamie, precisely because the strategy was to guard their privacy through the use of cliches. That is the reason we don't know nearly as much about Mamie's emotional life. And let me just say very quickly, that if Mamie had not written letters, indeed if these letters had not survived, we would not today be able to put together a full blown portrait of this woman.

In any case, the death of this first child was absolutely devastating for both of my grandparents. Think of how lucky we are as people who love history, and knowing a lot of these people, that we have a record of what this period was like in their lives. She writes:

Dearest Folksies,

Daddy's sweet letter came this morning and, oh, how good it did make me feel. I just had a feeling I would hear from someone each day. It seems good to be home but the emptiness sure does hurt. Just wandered around all morning. Ike and I didn't sleep an hour all Friday night.

This was just after the funeral and they'd returned from Denver, and the child was three and a half. In fact, they had an open casket which was traditional in the Doud family. The family sat up with the body and then buried this three year old next to her two sisters who had already died. A couple of days later she writes:

Dearest Folksies,

I do think the verse is the sweetest I've ever read. When I feel so badly, it helps me so much. I've read it a dozen times already. Ike and I had a very bad night last night. I just felt something would surely burst inside of me. I find the hardest time is when I go to bed and I can't tuck him in, and the many times I think I hear him in the night. I know I shouldn't write all this but I get so full up I have to tell someone and I know you all share my feelings and understand.

She signed the letter,

We feel like a couple of lost kids.

Ike, Mamie, and son, Ikky, in backyard of their home in Gettysburg, 1918. Captain Eisenhower was post commander of Camp Colt, the U.S. Army Tank Training Center in Gettysburg. (Dwight D. Eisenhower Library)

This great crisis did affect their marriage. There's no question about this. I think the sad thing was that Mamie was ready to talk about it. She wanted to face up to this issue in their relationship. On the other hand, I found a letter that Ike wrote to Nana in 1952. It said that his own view was that when people are hurt in their deepest selves, and shocked beyond all reckoning, the kindest thing that people can do is to allow that person privacy of heart and mind. And so, he was unable to talk about the death of his child and she really had no one to talk to herself. That's not to say that Ike did not recognize what kind of a tragedy this was for both of them. Nevertheless, there's no question that Mamie decided that she would have to put on a cheerful facade as a way to keep herself on an even keel. Ike later recalled that no matter what activities and preoccupations there were, "We could never forget the death of the boy." It was the one disaster from which, he said, he never fully recovered, and for Mamie, "the loss is heartbreaking and her grief, in turn, would have broken the hardest heart."

Historians think that this was the actual turning point in their marriage. And I think it had, no doubt, a great effect. But I also think that one of the problems in the historical community is people are too busy writing great stories and not necessarily doing the right kind of research. One of the things that I was moved by, in fact startled by, was a letter I found later that created a very, very different impression of how the death of this boy really affected the two. After Ikky died, and Ikky, by the way, was a nickname meaning little Ike. It was originally spelled Ikey, hinting at the origin. In an oral history that my mother took from Mamie before her death, it was very clear the derivation of this nickname.

In any case, after the death of this child, George Patton introduced Dwight Eisenhower to General Fox Connor, and Ike was given the opportunity to go to the Panama Canal Zone. Nearly every historical account says that Mamie went reluctantly, and when she got there she hated it, and that the marriage was in a real crisis. The interesting thing about what these letters reveal is quite the reverse. If you count nine fingers back from the moment of my father's birth, suddenly you discover that Mamie was two and one-half months pregnant when she went to the Panama Canal

Zone. Ike knew that she was pregnant at the time. Knowing what an act of love it was for this woman to say I'm two and a half months pregnant and I'm going to Panama, he volunteered to decline that position.

This was Panama, the Canal Zone, the disease infected Canal Zone of 1922. And indeed, this is a remarkable thing. One of the real surprises that led me to believe that was not the crisis in their marriage that every historical account suggested, was the letter I found that Ike had written Mamie dated June 3rd. I had to do a little detective work here, but it was very clear that it was the June 3 before my father's birth in August. Mamie had gone back to Denver where Ike joined her at the birth. But before doing so, he wrote her a letter that starts out "My sweet girl". He goes through a long list of his insurance policies and how much money the government owes him as a way to make sure that she would be protected in case anything happened to him. And then he says,

Now don't go wondering why I'm telling you all this. It's simply that I like to keep your memory refreshed on these things so you can get your dues in case of any accident. Because you see, dear, I love you. Much love to mother and Mike.

Your devoted lover.

Well, Mamie did go back to Denver. Ike joined her there, and my father was born. In fact, there is a wonderful story about how she went into labor. They liked to read out loud to each other at night. I think that very few people know that. He was reading her some short stories by Ring Lardner, and she got to laughing. He said, "You keep laughing like that and I'll be taking you to the hospital." She laughed so hard that her water broke. He was a nervous wreck and went out to get everybody organized because Nana wanted to go to the hospital too. He jumped into the car and put his foot hard on the accelerator and nothing happened. Mamie had to start the car first. In any case, my grandmother used to say that John was literally laughed into this world.

It is true that my grandparents' marriage went through difficulties during the Panama period. I think the historical community can't be faulted for thinking that there was trouble ahead. Mamie came back to the Zone with my father who was three or four months old and Ike was deeply absorbed in his work. He and Fox Connor were strategizing about the coming war. Fox Connor had Ike reading all kinds of books that would later become very important for his career.

But Mamie found herself left alone night after night as these two men talked about the forthcoming war. Then they'd go out on maneuvers, sometimes for five weeks at a time. Mamie was left alone in a set of quarters that had been built by the French and had been abandoned for ten years. It was a house that they finally just reconstructed by literally beating back the jungle. These quarters, when they first arrived there, were infested with snakes and bats. Monkeys from the jungle lived close to their house and they would scream in the night. Mamie said that at night, when she got up and walked around the porch of the house, she could hear the monkeys scream. She said, "And I felt like screaming, too."

When my father was probably a year or year and a half old, Mamie beat a retreat back to Denver. She sat in her parents' home and really tried to think about what this commitment to her husband meant. It wasn't that she didn't love this man, it was clear she did. But she understood that she had a very big choice to make. And let's not underestimate the size of that choice. Her parents were very wealthy and they were very protective. She could have gone home to Mama, and Mama would have been perfectly happy to take her in. But Mamie sat there and looked at her friends and she looked at her friends' husbands. They were doctors and lawyers. All of them came home at six or seven in the evening, and stayed all night. They seemed to have a normal life. But then as I say in my book, she realized that she wouldn't want to be married to any of them. So she made a decision to go back to the Panama Canal Zone with my father and to tough it out again. I think that she was deeply concerned that my father would get malaria, or some terrible disease, and she would lose a second child. This was clearly at the back of it. But she moved back and she recommitted herself in the fullest sense of the word. That crisis was averted.

Ike, Mamie, and John at Wyoming Apartments, Washington, D.C., c. 1930's. (Dwight D. Eisenhower Library)

After the Panama Canal Zone, there were many adventures ahead. Too many posts to mention in a short lecture like this. I think that perhaps the happiest time of their early marriage was the period spent at the Wyoming Apartments during the War Department years. This was a marvelous time. My father was between the age of five and twelve, maybe six and thirteen. He was in his golden years, that period before a child learns to talk back. She had the close proximity of many friends. It was amazing how many very important wartime figures all lived in the Wyoming Apartments at that time. They had a very, very close personal relationship.

Among the people who were there were the Gerows. Gee Gerow had actually introduced Ike and Mamie back in Fort Sam Houston and now he was living at the Wyoming with his wife, Katie. They had been with the Eisenhowers at Leavenworth. I think that one of the most moving parts of this book for me was what I learned about Mamie's relationship with Katie Gerow. If not for these letters, we would never have known the kind of friendship and loyalty Mamie felt for this woman. I think it says a tremendous amount about Mamie's character. The tragedy was that in 1934, Katie Gerow died of cancer. And again, Mamie had to deal with the death of one of the closest human beings to her. This was another great tragedy, and I think you'll find it of real interest that even decades after Katie Gerow's death, Mamie always had flowers sent to Arlington Cemetery. During the wartime years she kept Katie Gerow's picture right next to Ike's on her piano decades after this woman's death.

It was Katie Gerow's death from a cancer, which she had discovered in the Philippines, that created the next great crisis in the Eisenhower marriage. I'd like to read to you one of Mamie's letters to her parents about this terrible moment in her life. June 25, 1935 she says,

> I've had a terrible time trying to write this week. I just couldn't get my mind on it. Last Wednesday was Katie's funeral and after which I brought the family here for luncheon. It was so much better than letting them go back to the apartment. I have been over to see them this a.m.; they are still in a haze and poor Gee is sunk. All his friends are rallying around, but

there are so many hours when one has time to think.

It now looks like Ike will get his secret orders about September 17 for the Philippines, sailing about October 4th. We have talked and talked things over and have practically decided that John and I will stay on here in Washington until we see how the thing is going to turn out. John can finish his last grade school, which he is most anxious to do. I don't want to go over there, and in this way, at least one of us can have John.

I do hope you can come and stay with me, at least part of the time. It wouldn't pay me to move into a smaller apartment as rents have gone up so and it would mean storing a lot of things. Do you think you could come and be with me? This job may peter out, or Ike might not be able to stand the climate, and then we'd be in a mess. I hate to let him go alone, but he would live at the hotel. I don't want to go away so far from you all, and after Katie's experience, I'm scared. Of course, we still have a couple of months and something may happen to the whole thing.

I think that my grandmother believed that Katie Gerow had died from something that she had contracted in the Philippines and she was literally incapable of getting on a boat to be with her husband. I think one of the most dramatic parts of the story is that just before his departure to the Philippines, Ike wrote to his parents-in-law about his son John and says:

I miss him more this year than ever before. Possibly it's because I've got this Philippine thing staring me in the face and I realize we will be separated for many months at the very least. I hate the whole thought and I know that I'm going to be miserable. On the other hand, Mamie's so badly frightened, both for John and herself, at the prospect of going out there that I simply cannot urge her to go. My thoughts are that either I will be able to send her favorable reports as the conditions of health, education, etc. that she will be willing to come over next year, or that I will come home within a reasonably short time. I can only hope for the best, as the idea of being separated from my family has nothing for me but grief.

One of the big surprises in researching this book is that I didn't realize how passionately both of my grandparents felt, not only about each other, but also about these kinds of issues. Right after Ike got on a ship and left for the Philippines, he was writing plaintive letters to Mamie about his misery. For her birthday he sent four dozen, long stemmed roses. He enclosed a card saying, "Many happy returns of the day. So long as I live, I hope to be by your side on all your future birthdays. Much love, Ike." And then, Mamie wrote her parents. "They were exquisite", she told her mother. And the card read, "Each rose is a message of my devotion."

But Mamie was terribly miserable about this because she knew that she let Ike down. She wrote to her parents about great sadness, "He's terribly lonesome, said Shanghai was a trip for lovers, and the scenery was beautiful." So the next stage of the crisis in the Eisenhower marriage finally resolves itself when Mamie realizes that he is not coming home. She had to face up to the fact that she didn't go to the Philippines, and that this might be the end of things. So she went out and bought herself some new clothes, what they jokingly called her Philippine trousseau, and she went off to the Philippines. This was a very rocky period for some time. But within a fairly short period they had resolved their problems. In one of the most dramatic moments of self-reflection, Mamie told her parents to stop complaining that she was in the Philippines and would be gone for so long, saying simply, "I know how many mistakes I've made and it's up to me to rectify them."

Now this is all absolutely new information. The cliche used to guard their privacy was the cliche that John had to finish school. The truth of the matter was that Mamie was too frightened to go and I think this caused a really defining moment in the Eisenhower marriage.

They had gotten their marriage very much back on track during the later part of the Philippine tour. Ike was remarkable about remembering birthdays and Christmas.

Even years before at the Wyoming apartments, he saved his cigarette money to buy a tea service, piece by piece, for Mamie. He used his cigarette money to buy various pieces of silver. He lavished her with presents in the Philippines, so grateful he was that she had come to rejoin him.

So we move into the war period, and I think that this whole evolution of the Eisenhower marriage causes a lot of misunderstanding within the historical community. The truth of the matter is that by the time World War II came around, this marriage had absolutely stabilized. They had gone through these two crises, based around these hardship posts, and they came out of it much stronger than anyone can imagine. I think that is very important to understand before one gets into all the controversies of the World War II period. In fact, while Granddad was at War Plans, he was promoted to Marshall's number two. Mamie went to tremendous trouble to make a small apartment in Wardman Park available to the two of them, in a cozy, home-like way. Ike was just buoyed by the fact that she was there with him at this outset of the war. And again, contrary to everything we read about Mamie, she'd get up at six o'clock every morning and fix his breakfast. She fixed the breakfast, okay? She was tremendously supportive. So supportive in fact, that after he left for Europe, he wrote, "How I wish you were living here. You can't imagine how much you added to my efficiency in the hard months in Washington. Even I didn't realize it then, at least not fully. But I do now, and I'm grateful to you."

This marriage had become a partnership, a great team. And imagine what it was like saying good-bye to a husband who is to go off and take up this command at the time of the war when the outcome was far from certain. It could mean that overnight he might become a great American hero, or his decisions in the war might turn him into a symbol of failure.

I would just like to read you a section that I love in this book because this is such a wonderful example of how letters can create something for history that we just would never have from any other source. This is Mamie writing her letters about saying good-bye to her husband, adopting an uncertain future, and sending a husband off to fight the worst war the world had ever seen.

I should say very quickly that my father had come from West Point that weekend to say good-bye to his father. During those days they spent a tremendous amount of time together. Then Ike and Mamie had two days alone before his departure for Europe. Well, Ike couldn't go to the airfield to see John off so Mamie and her friend, Kitty Smith, were set to ride with John to Bolling Air Force Base. Mamie wrote to her parents about John's going back to West Point before Ike's departure for Europe. She described his departure from Quarters Seven:

> Picture Ike standing on the steps, John beside the car at the curb. John faces his father and gives a snappy salute, one soldier to another. Poor John's Adams apple was sure churning up and down as he turned the corner.

In the last two days, Ike and Mamie had time together. Then they had a deal that Ike would leave on a plane, and she would run out to the flagpole there at Fort Myer, and wave good-bye. So she writes: "The last thing he did was reach out of the car and kiss my hand, saying with a broad grin, 'Good-bye, honey.'" Ike told the pilot that after take-off he wanted the plane to fly back over Fort Myer for one last look. Mamie had promised that she would be at the flag pole. The airfield called Mamie when Ike's plane was ready. Remembering how quickly the departure from Washington could be, Mamie with two friends who had come to keep her company and lend support, literally flew across the clipped lawn to a spot beside the flag pole. But the wind conditions required that the plane turn northward after it crossed the Potomac away from Fort Myer. All the same, Mamie could see the aircraft clearly as it headed away. She and her companions yelled, "Happy landings."

Mamie had dinner that night with friends at Fort Myer, and received messages of the plane's whereabouts all evening long. Just before she went home, she got word that the plane was over the ocean and that they were really "on their way." She writes to her parents, "I'll have to admit I felt pretty low when I crawled into bed knowing that my darling was God knew where, though I didn't cry at all." The next morning Mamie received a message that the bird had landed and several days later she had a cable from Ike himself. "Because of you I have been the luckiest of men in the world for 26 years. Love, Ike."

And so the war began for Ike in the most real of all ways. He took up his command at headquarters. This was really going to be a trial of another kind in this marriage because, in fact, Mamie was Mrs. Commander. She had the wives of Ike's subordinates living in the same apartment building with her. There were all kinds of challenges associated with trying to keep the morale up. He felt that was one of the chief jobs of his command, that is, keeping up the level of optimism with the troops at all times.

I think that very few historians realize how well developed their team work had been. During the war, Ike had told Mamie very clearly that he was going to lead a very quiet life. And this is what turned out to be the case. Ike had his own rule that he would never go out during the war and be seen in public until the war was over. Much more dramatic was that Mamie adopted exactly the same position. Throughout the entire three year period of the war, Mamie did not go out once in public, unless it was an official occasion. She said that she did not want to be seen in restaurants with alcohol on the table and people laughing while her husband sent their sons off to their deaths. I think that this was a very dramatic thing. The sad part of this story is that the gossip mongers of Washington and people who were threatened by Eisenhower's popularity misunderstood her absences from public places.

Simultaneous with Mamie's decision to stay and lead a very quiet life during the Wardman period, was the discovery of Mamie's Menieres syndrome, which is an inner ear disorder that causes misbalance and an unsteady gait. This, of course, has been a subject of much discussion over the years. It was this inner ear disorder that caused malicious gossip to rise that Mamie had a drinking problem, which, of course, was not the case.

I know that we can get into many more aspects of this war time period. I certainly have not skirted any with respect to my grandfather's relationship with Kay Summersby in this book. I think it's a very, very important thing to go through because I found absolutely no evidence for a romance in any of the correspondence or among the witnesses to life at headquarters. I had a remarkable experience of running across my grandfather's wartime secretary in the last few years. There were three of them during the war. I think two of them are dead and one is still very much alive. We met one another at the 50th Anniversary of D-day celebrations. When I realized that she had been with my grandfather from the North African period all the way through Chief-of-Staff of the Army period, I understood that she might be able to help me with this question. So one evening I said, "Sue, do you think we could have breakfast tomorrow morning and talk about something?" Well, I don't know whether she was expecting the question or not, but I asked her directly. I said, "You know, it's not going to hurt my feelings if Dwight Eisenhower had a romantic relationship with another woman for the simple fact that I don't think there's anybody who could pass judgement on a man who had literally the weight of the world on his shoulders and was separated from his wife for three solid years."

Of course there was the famous quotation of one of his generals, "Who cares whether Eisenhower's involved with Summersby, she's helping him win the war." That was the attitude of many people and would have been my attitude, too.

Sue told me that she would go to her grave worrying about this issue. She said that Eisenhower and Summersby were just good friends. He was a highly disciplined man. Kay had been engaged to someone else and there was a kind of hero worship at headquarters. The truth was that there was no relationship. She told me several other things which are crucial to this question. Maybe the most important of which is that it was not Eisenhower's idea to make Kay Summersby his aide. It was Kay's friend, Sue, who I talked to. She suggested that Kay become an aide to Eisenhower because it would bring $15 more per month in her paycheck. This will remain a controversial issue. I say with some sadness that I feel the necessity to stand up here and go through this chapter and verse. I hope that the tremendous amount of material that I've amassed here will finally put this issue to rest. I personally look forward to the next book on Mamie Eisenhower when we won't have to go through this. Or if we do, we will do so in a minimal way. The way I handled it in this book, was to raise the question of

Summersby whenever I felt it directly affected my grandmother's happiness, or whenever I thought it entered her thoughts. Unfortunately there had to be more than one section on this issue in the book. As you all know, during my grandmother's later years there was a controversy that was started by Harry Truman in 1973 about whether Ike had intentions to divorce Mamie. This came to the fore and the next thing we had was a book, a second book promised by Mrs. Summersby which was eventually called *Past Forgetting; My Love Affair with Dwight Eisenhower.*

You might be surprised to know that Kay Summersby never really wrote the book. And never saw the manuscript. She died within one month of signing the book contract and the book was written by a number of ghost writers.

Perhaps even more surprising is that a television miniseries produced a multi-part program based on the book written by the person who never saw the manuscript. The result is that this particular episode became part of the pop-culture. I think that Dr. Marling would agree with that. She's our expert on popular culture. The tragedy is, I think, very simple. This rumor was used for political purposes. I have interviewed people who were there when it was being spread during the '52 campaign and before as a pre-emptive strike. I think it was used for political purposes and today it's being used for political purposes. The reason I hope it's cleared up is not because it makes that much difference to me, because I know my grandfather loved my grandmother. It's so evident in all his wartime letters, and you'll read that for yourself in the book. But the tragedy is that we have given the impression to our kids today that there is not one public figure that they can look up to as being somebody worthy of respect, a person with the kind of family values that they espouse.

And so, it was a great privilege to me to do this kind of research. I was spurred on very, very strongly by these letters I found, and the ability to put it together chronologically. Mamie was the first to say, "We had our problems in our marriage," but I see this book, as I hope the rest of the American public will see this book, as finally a celebration of a marriage. A celebration of what it means to stay together, what it means to build a life over a 53 year period. What it means is so much more important than all the aspects of gossip that everybody wants to concentrate on. The story I wrote is not one of smooth sailing or total bliss. It's a story of two human beings who cared about each other and chose to take the tough road and to stay together.

I would like to close by reading you the letter that convinced me that I had to write this book. I discovered this letter, believe it or not, sitting in a pile of papers. I even wonder whether Mamie ever saw this letter. I don't know, because the letter itself was supposed to be opened by Mamie only in case of accident, or death, to Dwight Eisenhower during World War II. I understood the minute I started reading it that this was more important than all of the other letters he wrote during the war. On the outside of the envelope, it said "Censored by..." and he had written his own name. In any case, it's written July 1, 1943. It says:

Darling Girl,

I hope you never have to read this note because it's kept in an envelope that is to be opened only in case of accident to me. But if such should happen, you'll receive this way at least one more assurance that I love you only, that I have been a most fortunate man in having you for my wife, and that I'm proud of our son. I love him so much that I follow every word he writes to me with curious intensity. He is what he is only because he had you for a mother. So do not grieve if I go out in this war. I hope that I will have left a name of which you need not be ashamed and that it will be universally acknowledged that I did my duty to the best of my ability. Spend no time mourning and you can still make a number of people happy in this world. And that is the surest way to your own happiness.

With all my love, always,

Your lover for all these years